What C

Written by Margaret Clyne
and Rachel Griffiths

Illustrated by Linda Ayriss

A polar bear can catch fish under the ice.

I can catch fish too,
but not like a polar bear!

A fox can hide
in the snow.

I can hide too,
but not like a fox.

A seal can swim fast
in the sea.

I can swim too,
but not like a seal.

But I can float
like a sea otter.

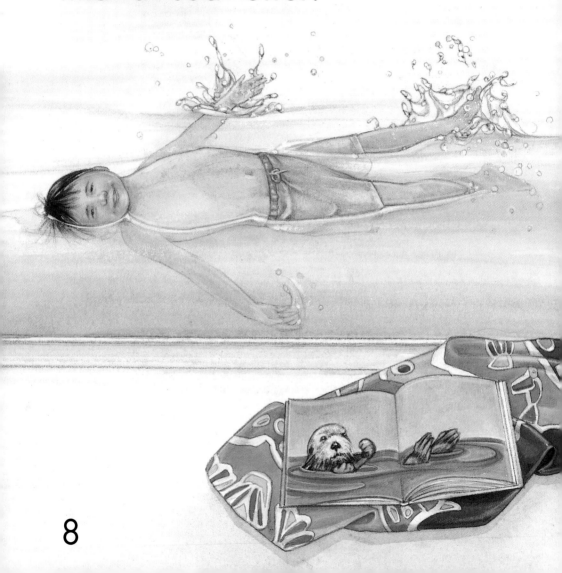